ONE HUNDRED KISSES FOR TONI

BY

DAVE GOODWIN

FOREWORD

I was born and brought up in Liverpool, one of seven brothers, no sisters. I lived in a town called Kirkby and am back there now. Because of my job as a contracting mechanical engineer, I travelled the country, causing an absence of 22 years in South Wales, where I lived in a village called Pyle, just outside of Bridgend. I also lived in Newark, Nottingham, for a while, approximately 3½ years on and off.

It was while I was living there, I was stabbed and almost died. I was attacked from behind and stabbed in the right shoulder when I turned, and I had a meat fork put through my right eye and into my brain. Making a bad decision to go down to the floor because the room was spinning, I was then stamped on and kicked to the head and body, causing, amongst other injuries, a fractured skull. Nice, eh? It was my then partner and a member of her family who were the attackers. So it's true, see? Men do suffer domestic abuse.

These poems were originally written to a special person, who has helped me and is still helping me recover. The writing of them has helped me and I hope the reading of them will in some way help the reader.

I have read a lot of poetry in my 56 years of life; if I've duplicated any line or verse, I assure you it hasn't been intentional so please forgive me. I sincerely hope you enjoy part of my mind.

When I was on the floor after being beaten and stabbed to my shoulder and through my right eye into my brain, and was continuously being kicked and stamped on to my head, I thought I heard myself saying, "Get up, get up. If you don't get up they'll kill you." Since then, a spiritualist has told me I wasn't saying this, it was my dead brother shouting at me. Believe it or not, it's entirely up to you. So for all my brothers, my children and grandchildren, and my mother and Toni, this is especially for you.

DEDICATION

1. FOR MY BROTHERS

Brothers Poem

Seven lights all born from one womb
Shone so bright to fill a room
Separate paths they all blazed
Until one faulted in a haze.

Through pain and suffering you went out
And left the rest in no doubt
That one day we'll meet again
In that place on a heavenly plain.

Until that day we'll shine through
In heads and hearts we'll remember you.

You've gone to a place we don't know
You'll blaze a path that we must go
So ignite your light on the other side
For when we follow you must guide.

Until that day when we meet again
In our heads and hearts you'll remain

When the dust has settled and we must cry
The sobs of grief you cannot deny.

Heartfelt anguish heartfelt pain
Will disappear when we meet again.

*

2. FOR MY COMRADES

Guns and flashes explosions through the night
We knew we were in a terrible fight
Frightened and shaking we were trapped there
Some of the boys were in total despair.

The battle raged on, people screaming I hear
It was building inside, a terrible fear
Then with a bang, a bright flash of light
Oh no my friend… His clothing alight.

I tried to save him, he's in terrible pain
But I couldn't get there, the bullets again
Zipping and pinging past my body as closer I move
The bullets don't stop, I can't get there to soothe.

The screams seemed to last forever
But they never I'm told
It was then that my body
Turned totally cold.

"Up and at them," I heard the scream
Running towards them, like in a dream
Bayonets fixed
I still see the scene.

The next bit's not nice
A terrible sight
Suffice is to say
We won that bloody fight.

My mind goes back to that terrible day
I'm not proud, but I have to say
If I hadn't done what I did that day
I wouldn't be here to love you this way.

*

3. FOR MY UNCLES

Uncle Knight

You always had more time for me
Than anyone else, as far as I could see
You made me feel when you where there
That I was wanted and you did care.

You protected me, when no one would
You showed me love and I felt good
You held my hand when I was afraid
From that day on a bond was made.

Never a mention throughout my life
That you were my protector
My own true Knight.

So go to a place that's been reserved
On solemn ground that you deserve
Goodnight, God bless, and you sleep tight
My uncle Jack

My own Sir Knight.

*

ONE HUNDRED KISSES FOR TONI

CONTENTS

1. Warming My Heart.. 1

2. Forever My Friend... 2

3. Can't You Tell?.. 3

4. Deeply.. 4

5. My Body Pets... 5

6. Caring of Generations 7

7. Proud of You... 9

8. Goodnight 11

9. You and I 12

10. I Love You 13

11. A Little Bit... 14

12. You.. 16

13. Mummy Guide 18

14. Crazy... 19

15. Mine.. 20

16. A Kiss... 21

17. Finding You 22

18. Waiting 23

19. I Want 24

20. Plans 25

21. With Me... 26

22. Happy 27

23. Heart of Gold... 28

24. I'm Only 29

25. Dream My Dreams... 30

26. Bottle 31

27. More Than More 32

28. Sometimes 33

29. Sorry..34

30. Thank You..35

31. Thought..36

32. Toni...37

33. You Are..39

34. I'll Wait..41

35. Lather..42

36. I Love..43

37. You and Me...44

38. Someone Special..45

39. Our Future..46

40. Fear..47

41. Our Poem...49

42. Forever..50

43. Patient Love..52

44. Perfect...53

45. Nightmare..54

46. Pain..55

47. Loneliness..57

48. Dreams..58

49. Our First New Day..59

50. Struggle...60

51. Cosy...61

52. Dreaming of Kisses...62

53. Keepsakes..63

54. Feelings...64

55. Explain..66

56. Wishes and Dreams..67

57. I Love..68

58. I'll Be There for You..69

59. Mother's Always Here..72

60. Vision..74

61. My Angel 75

62. Thank You.. 76

63. Near Tomorrow 77

64. Courage.. 79

65. All the World to See 80

66. No Promises 82

67. You Are 83

68. Over and Over 84

69. With You 85

70. Loneliness 86

71. No Matter 87

72. Miracle 88

73. Did I Mention?.. 89

74. I Could 91

75. The One.. 93

76. You Are 94

77. Intention 95

78. My Search for You.................................... 96

79. Truly Feels.. 97

80. Picture in My Mind.................................. 98

81. Society.. 99

82. Stay Calm.. 101

83. I Love You 102

84. Any Parent to Any Child.......................... 103

85. Exercise 105

86. Pink Day 106

87. Shout and Sing 108

88. Determination.. 109

89. Keeping you Safe 110

90. Million.. 111

91. Magic Wand.. 112

92. It's You 113

93. Very Sorry...114
94. Weather..115
95. Speaking...116
96. I'll Love You 118
97. Healing a Heart 119
98. Mention 121
99. Mothers..122
100. Together We Can...124

ACKNOWLEDGMENTS

Everyone who has helped in not only the writing of *One Hundred Kisses for Toni*, but also those too numerous to mention in my ongoing recovery.

1. *Warming My Heart*

My heart was broken and turned cold as ice
When the woman I loved stabbed me twice
I was set for a future baron and bare
No warmth left in me, cold and ice was there.

I saw a blonde angel floating around the ward
With a smile that was amazing, happy and broad
Her eyes lit up shiny and bright
The ice began to melt at first sight.

I never thought I'd care anymore
Until I saw this angel, then the ice did thaw
But she's taken and happy, she told me so
Though the warmth inside me continues to grow.

Friends for life is all we'll be
And that suits me fine, cos you see
I'm alive again and happy to be
Your friend for life, with a heart warm and free.

2. Forever My Friend

We all need someone
To talk to in our life
A friend to whom we run
In times of stress and strife.

A friend who's always there
Throughout the years
A friend we know will care
And take away our fears.

A friend who's always near
Waiting for our call
To wipe away the tears
And lift us when we fall.

A loving friend indeed
On whom we can depend
To fulfil our every need
Thank you precious friend.

3. Can't You Tell?

I didn't feel much like anything
I didn't feel much like much
I didn't want to carry on
Till I felt your loving touch

Your eyes were shiny and magical
A glint was in your stare
As soon as I looked into them
I knew that love was there

Your smile is kind and caring
With it I can tell
Love is there and with your stare
For them I'd walk through hell

I'm not the type of person
To open my heart at all
But for you I swear, I'll always be there
Until the heavens fall

You are my perfect angel
And in my heart you'll dwell
Beautiful, sexy and wonderful
I love you, can't you tell?

4. Deeply

From the moment I wake up
Till the time I go to sleep
Even in my dreams
My love for you runs deep.

It runs deeper than the ocean
It runs deeper than the sea
Each day that I miss you
I will make it up by three.

If it takes my whole life
Till the day I pass away
I'll make sure to keep you happy
Each and every day.

When I finally get to see you
Your beautiful face aglow
I'm going to hold you in my arms
And never let you go.

The day I get you home
I won't know what to do
But one thing I do know
I'm deeply in love with you.

5. My Body Pets

With a Tiger on the left
And a Lion on the right
Covering my back
A Unicorn takes flight.

A pink Rose covers my heart
With your name as the stem
Right from the start
My pets will protect them.

It's like life itself
They protect my health
No pain anymore
As they start to roar.

So I will always be here
When in life you fear
So don't despair
My pets and I will always be there.

You've captured my heart
With the glint in your eye
The smile on your face
Lets me know you can't lie.

I just want to end
By telling you this
Our life together
Will be eternal bliss.

6. Caring of Generations

Sometimes our lives are difficult
And nothing seems to go right
It's at the times of uncertainty
That we have to stand and fight.

We help, we feed, we nurture
Our children from their birth
And mostly we'll do anything
To tell them what they're worth.

Sometimes when they are hurting
We feel the pain with them
But when they are elated
We are just as happy and then.

They grow and as time passes
They leave us all behind
We've watched them through all classes
We've seen them learn and climb.

And then they meet that someone
That someone special to them
We find ourselves all lonely
And worrying all over again.

So look at life like this
With happiness love and bliss
It's then they have their turn
Of watching their children learn.

7. Proud of You

Deep breath in
Blow it all out
Come up to the line
You hear them shout.

Bang of the gun
And off we go
Pounding the road
The pace is slow.

Look to the left
Look to the right
Runners all around
It's a wonderful sight.

You're bounding along
Not quite full speed
You're holding it back
There's more if you need.

Moving on through
Picking up speed
Passing the stragglers
Closing on the lead.

Closing up fast
Beginning to believe
If you push a bit more
You'll soon take the lead.

Beginning to pound
Your heart beats away
Could this be your chance
Of winning today?

Neck and neck
Up with the lead
Your lungs are burning
More oxygen they need.

The line's closing in
You can see it, it's there
Legs are pounding
Arms pumping air.

One last push
You have to this day
You'll be a champion
Forever they'll say.

You did it yourself
With guts, power and drive
A wonderful race
So happy you tried.

Didn't finish first
But a champion you'll be
Cos you ran to beat cancer
How wonderful to see.

8. Goodnight

So now it's time to say goodnight
Don't forget to switch off the light
And in your dreams I'll be there
With a tender kiss and loving care.

We'll meet there when you are asleep, you see
And dream of things that are meant to be
Together in love you and me
In each other's arms for all eternity.

"It's only a dream," I hear you say
But I will wait till my dying day
Cos in my heart forever you'll stay
I'll cherish you in a loving way.

It's written in the stars bold and clear
Our time together is drawing near
I know it's close it's in my heart
We're both in love and we'll never part.

9. You and I

I could sing lyrics from my heart
You must have noticed right from the start
I could tell you I love you in rhyme and song
But it wouldn't matter, you knew all along.

But still I say I'll always be there
With kisses and hugs and tender care
You captured my heart with a smile and a sigh
We will be in love for all time, you and I.

10. I Love You

I love you I love you
I have to say
I love you tomorrow
I love you today.

I love you when near
I love you when far
Don't get the bus
When you can be in my car.

I would be happy
And you would be too
So come drive with me
We'll find plenty to do.

11. A Little Bit

A little bit older
A little bit sad
A little bit crazy
A little bit mad.

A little bit this
A little bit that
A little bit loved
As a matter of fact.

A little bit high
A little bit low
A little bit shy
I'm sure you know.

A little bit clever
A little bit wise
I can see your smile
And those amazing eyes.

A little bit happy
A little bit glad
A little bit naughty
And a little bit bad.

Little of all
These wonderful things
Makes me so happy
With the joy that it brings.

A little bit you
A little bit me
Makes love forever
And always you'll see.

12. You

You opened my heart
When it was closed
You made it warm
When it was stone cold.

You made me happy
When I was sad
You proved to me
Life's not all bad.

You made me realise
That I'd be ok
You make me think
With the things that you say.

You make my heart
Beat faster again
The light of my soul
Is brighter and then.

You smile at me
Then I can see
Life is worth living
And someone wants me.

I thought for a long time
That I'd remain alone
Sad and so lonely
In my own home.

Then I saw you
You made my heart soar
I've never been in love
Like this before.

You're beautiful and happy
And wonderful to me
You opened my eyes
Now I can see.

You gave me your trust
You gave me your heart
I'll love you forever
And we'll never part.

When light turns to dark
And day turns to night
I know we've found love
That's pure and so right.

Never again
Through all eternity
Will I feel alone
Cos you are with me.

Happily ever after it will be
For you and me baby, you will see
You're in my heart, you're in my mind
We'll be together, till the end of time.

13. Mummy Guide

What a wonderful little girl
So happy she must be
Running around and around
Just like her lovely mummy.

She borrows your high heels
She tells you how she feels
To copy you by day
When she's happy in her play.

She goes asleep at night
Dreaming eyes closed tight
Of Mummy playing games
And helping when she trains.

You're teaching her to grow
And in time you will know
What a kind and gentle girl
You've brought into this world.

And as time passes by
You'll remember with a sigh
What an amazing wonderful guide
Your child has by her side.

14. Crazy

Crazily crazy
Crazily nice
Too crazy indeed
To take good advice.

Crazy when I chef
Crazy when I dance
Crazy in love
Crazy for romance.

Crazy when I laugh
Crazy when I cry
Crazy for you
We'll never say goodbye.

I'm crazy right now
My crazy little heart
Is crazy in love
With you from the start.

15. Mine

Whilst you sit there drinking
And having a little fun
I'll be here just thinking
About what we have done.

We've found each other at last
And looking through my past
I've waited a long time
To finally make you mine.

16. A Kiss

Though at the moment
We are apart
In my thoughts
You are in my heart.

Each moment I think of you
Though you are not near
I have a wish
For you my dear.

In our life ahead
May your dreams come true
And know for sure
My love for you is true.

May you always get
Love and peace of mind
And wonderful kisses
From who you got in mind.

May your day ahead
End with bliss
And a loving hug
Then from me a kiss.

17. Finding You

Because I want to see you
I've driven around the town
Around and around and up and down
The same old lane I found.

I couldn't fine the bus stop
You said that you were at
I was getting pretty worried
I thought my tyres were flat.

I couldn't seem to get there
Or find you anywhere
Then I seen it, there it is
I found the pub Clubmoor.

I went a little further
And saw to my surprise
A beautiful sexy angel
With shining glowing eyes.

18. Waiting

I'm just sitting here
Waiting you see
For a beautiful angel
To meet me.

I can hardly believe
I'm so happy to be
Waiting here
For my angel to see.

I'm excited I've found
My heart begins to pound
At the vision of her
And the love I've found.

See her everyday
And I'm so pleased to say
I'll love her forever
Always and a day.

19. I Want

I want to hold you
And kiss those lovely lips
I want to feel your heartbeat
Through my fingertips.

I want you here forever
Always by my side
With loving truth and honesty
You'll be my beautiful bride.

I'll love you all my lifetime
Forever and a day
And when it's time to go
I'll beg, Lord let me stay.

I want to be with you
My true love
My soulmate
My beautiful bride.

I'll be with you forever
My heart
My soul
My pride.

20. Plans

Beautiful and sexy
That's what you are
I often tell you
When sitting in my car.

The thought of us together
Lights up my life
I'll love you forever
I'll make you my wife.

The plans and the dreams
We have sitting there
Makes my life so worthwhile
Wonderful and with care.

I know it's in the future
Our life will be together
I have to tell you baby
For us it's always and forever.

21. With Me

I have hoped
Right from the start
To be with you
And never to part.

We'll live a life
Of love and joy
Always and forever
This girl and this boy.

Our love will grow stronger
As time goes by
We'll share together
Such comfort and joy.

I'll be with you
And you will see
What love's really like
Forever with me.

22. Happy

I am happy
To say to you
Whatever you want
I'll do for you.

A kiss in the morning
A long kiss goodnight
Enclosed in my arms
I'll make everything alright.

We'll live a happy
And wonderful life
You'll make me so proud
You'll become my wife.

Loving and caring
That's what we'll be
You've captured my heart
For all eternity.

23. Heart of Gold

You have a heart of precious gold
One that's pure and true
You show your love and caring
In everything you do.

Just like your loving heart of gold
Your spirit always shines
Bringing joy to those you love
I'm so proud to call you mine.

24. I'm Only

I'm only a little bit crazy
I'm only a little bit mad
I'm always gonna be happy
I'm never gonna be sad.

I'm only a little bit loopy
I'm only a little bit nuts
I'll always be our cutie
I'll never be a klutz.

You'll always be my angel
You'll always be my pride
You'll always make me happy
One day you'll be my bride.

25. Dream My Dreams

I could sit here and dream
I would dream my dreams of you
I would dream that in real life
You are my wonderful wife.

I'd make you very happy
We'd have a wonderful life
We'd cuddle up together
And be in love forever.

With you here by my side
My heart would fill with pride
The happiness we feel
Because we know this love is real.

26. Bottle

I wish I was a bottle
A bottle full of ale
I'd drip in bits right through your lips
And down your throat I'd sail.

I'd make you feel all fuzzy
And happy from inside
You'd drink a little more and begin to adore
The happiness I provide.

But I am not a bottle
A bottle full of ale
But I'm still here without the beer
Cos true love will never fail.

27. More Than More

My love for you is eternal
My heart beats out of sight
Those amazing eyes and beautiful smile
Tell me that I'm right.

I love you more than more
My heart it tells me so
I know that when I hold you
I never want to let you go.

I know that when I'm with you
My heart begins to soar
So listen when I tell you
I love you more than more.

More than more forever
I know my heart it says
When we are together
I will love you for always.

28. Sometimes

Sometimes we're lonely
Sometimes we're down
Our feelings are obvious
We see it in our frown.

We don't want to talk
Or sit and explain
Nobody would like it
If they felt our pain.

But just remember that
You're intelligent and kind
A person like you
Is so hard to find.

Your beautiful smile
Is often the cure
You can get through anything
Of that I'm sure.

Please remember
I'm here for you
I care for you dearly
And my love for you is true.

29. Sorry

I don't know what to do
I don't know what to say
I didn't take my phone
On the roof today.

I'm sorry if I hurt you
I'm sorry I didn't say
I wouldn't have my phone
On the roof today.

I'm really really sorry
I caused you to worry
I tried to finish the job
In a real big hurry.

I wasn't really thinking
I wasn't being kind
I should have known
You'd have me on your mind.

So I'm sorry that I'm thoughtless
I wasn't very kind
I'm sorry sorry sorry
I'm sorry for all time.

30. Thank You

Thank you for accepting
My apologies
I didn't really want to
Cause unnecessary worries.

Don't want you to be sad
Definitely not upset
I'll try to make you happy
Next time I won't forget.

I love you very dearly
And I always will try
To eliminate all worries
Until the day I die.

31. Thought

My heart is bleeding
It's hurting it's broken
It's full of feeling
It's always hoping
And dreaming of you
Is my way of coping.

32. Toni

Before I wake
I always dream
About the woman
That will be my queen.

She's sexy, pretty
And full of life
This is the woman
I'll make my wife.

Before I met her
My life was lonely
That's why I'm so glad
That I met Toni.

We will get married
She'll be my wife
She'll be happy
The love of my life.

I will tell her
Every single day
How much I love her
I'm here to stay.

She's the perfect
Partner for me
Our love will go on
For all eternity.

33. You Are

You're as lovely as the flowers
That are blooming in the spring
You're as fresh as all the petals
That's been washed by gentle rain.

You're as bright as rays of sunshine
That clears the rain away
You're a part of everything
That makes my perfect day.

You're as lovely as the winter
When snow is on the ground
Although the smell of summer has gone
And flowers aren't around.

You brighten up the skies
When clouds turn them grey
You are part of everything
That makes my perfect day.

You're always with me in my heart
No matter where you go
And whether near or far apart
I wanted you to know.

The best way I can tell you
Is to come right out and say
I will love you always
Forever every day.

34. I'll Wait

My patience has no end
When it comes to loving you
And I will wait a lifetime
Just to be with you.

Real love doesn't go away
It doesn't pass or fade
It goes on forever
And ours will, always.

I will wait a lifetime
Because you are my soul
And behind all the doubt
I know we can't let go.

You are my soul
And I am yours
If two people were meant to be
It's definitely you and me.

35. Lather

I wish I was a bubble
I wish I was soap
Cos lying in there next to you
Is my dream and hope.

I'd rub myself all over you
I'd have you in a lather
With soap and bubbles and hugs and cuddles
It's happy ever after.

36. I Love

I love you with all my heart
I love you with all my soul
I aim to make you happy
Well that's my goal.

I love it when you're happy
I love to see you glad
When someone upsets you
It makes me really mad.

I promise to protect you
To love you all my life
To kiss and cuddle and comfort you
And take you for my wife.

37. You and Me

It's you and me
Forever you see
In love for
All eternity.

I miss you so much
When you're not there
I love you deeply
I truly care.

In dark nights
And long bright days
We will be in love
Forever and always.

38. Someone Special

All the beauty on earth
Will never compare
To that look in your eyes
When I look in there.

My heart rate increases
And you fuel each beat
With that wonderful smile
And amazing eyes, every time we meet.

We share more than love
We naturally connect
Be safe in these arms
You I'll always protect.

You're someone special
Thoughtful and kind
The very centre
Of my heart and mind.

39. Our Future

For all eternity
Into your eyes I could stare
That shining glint of happiness
Tells me love is there.

I promise to be patient
I passionately believe
There's nothing in this world
We cannot achieve.

Our love is truly magical
Our bond is stronger than steel
The dreams that we share
Will soon be real.

To each of my days
Happiness you bring
Because of your love
My heart has learned to sing.

Where our future will take us
I haven't got a clue
But I just can't wait
To spend it with you.

40. Fear

I fear the struggle
I fear the strife
A fear of dream
A fear of life.

I fear for you
I fear for me
I fear of what
Will come to be.

There's plenty to fear
Than fear itself
I fear of pain
And fear poor health.

I fear my well
Is running dry
I fear so much
I'm forced to cry.

I fear disaster
I fear a knife
I fear the blade
That is my life.

I fear the man
I came to be
I fear the dark
I fail to see.

I fear life left me
On the shelf
I fear so much
It harms my health.

I fear the help
For which I cry
I fear success
I'm scared to try.

Fear is nothing
It's in my head
I think I'll live life
And be happy instead.

41. Our Poem

I know the pressure
And pain you feel
No one can help
When love is real.

Life isn't perfect
Good things are few
The only thing good
In my life is you.

I know you love me
I see it in your eyes
That's why when I hold you
It's for the rest of our lives.

42. Forever

Forever takes a minute
While I'm here with you
I'm falling even more in love
With everything you do.

Hold me in your arms
Look deep into my eyes
Don't turn away and let me go
Don't ever say goodbyes.

I swear I'll never leave you
In my arms I'll always hold
I'll never let you slip away
Or leave nothing untold.

There aren't enough hours
In every passing day
To find all the words
I wish I could say.

Your kiss will last forever
Your touch forever warm
I'll guide you to the sunlight
And shield you from the storm.

This is what I'm saying
With everything that's true
I swear to all in heaven
I really do love you.

43. Patient Love

Love is patient with a life
That brings its share of pain
We know sometimes there is an end
To the most stubborn rain.

We know the sun comes out again
On a world that's fresh and new
And all the gifts we freely give
Somewhere, sometime accrue.

We know sometimes we have to wait
For life to come around
And sometimes that it won't, but still
There's some good to be found.

And even when things happen
That your soul can hardly bear
Know that I'll be next to you
My love is always there.

44. Perfect

Perfectly happy
Perfectly nice
Perfectly perfect
I said it twice.

Perfectly lovely
Perfectly sexy
Perfectly perfect
Even on a txt see.

Perfectly wonderful
You're perfectly you
Perfectly perfect
And I love you.

45. Nightmare

When asleep and dreaming
The lion attacks
Trying to tell me
To look at the facts.

It's fighting me now
It's got something to say
Until I face it
It won't go away.

I struggle to win
A hard-fought fight
My life will begin
Cos I know that I'm right.

The lion has lost
And I won't count the cost
Of a battle I fought
To get my day in court.

46. Pain

The moment I saw you cry
My world came crashing down
To see those tears fall from your eyes
Turned my smile into a frown.

I wanted to hold you
Make everything alright
But there was nothing I could do
To stop you from crying that night.

I felt like a failure
To myself and you
But you said there was nothing
That I could do.

I held you close
And made your pain my own
I tried to make you feel
That you weren't alone.

You kissed me softly
Said you would be alright
But there was something in your eyes
That had me worried that night.

And to this day I promise
Not to let you cry alone
And to take all the pain you feel
And make it my own.

47. Loneliness

A lonely tear falls down
A smile turns to a frown
Trickles down the cheek
Does not make you weak.

A lonely tear escapes
A lifetime of mistakes
A sad and lonely heart
That others broke apart.

A lonely tear is dried
So many nights it cried
A friend reached out a hand
And tried to understand.

The lonely tear has gone
Life will carry on
With love from a friend
The lonely tears will end.

48. Dreams

You brought sunshine
When I only saw rain
You brought me laughter
When I only felt rain.

Romantics at heart
Love at first sight
Have I known you before?
God, this feels so right.

Have I met you before?
Another time, another place
Just to make you happy
To see a smile upon your face.

I want you to know
Cos I'll never forget
Knowing your smile
Your eyes and yet.

Dreams are something
That sometimes come true
That's why I'm saying
I'm in love with you.

49. Our First New Day

Greet the bright dawn with joy
Raise your spirit to the light
Then your smile you must employ
Swiftly expelling the gloomy night.

A new day comes into view
To be shaped and to redesign
And each move will be by you
So perfect, so right and fine.

The birds will start their song
And delight in this new day
And with your courage so strong
Exhilaration will come your way.

Greet the bright dawn with joy
Don't give in to tears and stress
Find nothing that might annoy
Come to know complete happiness.

50. Struggle

You may see me struggle
But you won't see me fall
Regardless If I'm weak or not
I'm going to stand tall.

Everyone says life is easy
But clearly living is not
Times get hard, people struggle
And constantly get put on the spot.

I'm going to wear my biggest smile
Even though I want to cry
I'm going to fight to live
Even though I'm destined to die.

And even though it's hard
And I may struggle through it all
You may see me struggle
But you will never see me fall.

51. Cosy

Dim the lights within the room
From bright to subtle glow
Put our favourite CD on
Turn the pace from fast to slow.

Arrange the cushions on the couch
Fur throw to warm your toes
Then we cuddle up so tight
To see how the evening goes.

The music takes the stress away
With a nice cool glass of wine
Let your worries drift along
As I do the same with mine.

All relaxed and fully chilled
The wine has made me heady
Try as I might to pour some more
My hands become unsteady.

Cosy up together close
I'll kiss your ruby lips
And we can stay forevermore
In lasting love and bliss.

52. Dreaming of Kisses

I meet your gaze, I help you stand
I hold my breath and kiss your hand
I see you blush your cheeks red now
I smell your hair and kiss your brow.

It brings me joy to hear you speak
I take your hand and kiss your cheek
I feel your skin with my fingertips
I hold your face and kiss your lips.

Our love's true passion now begins
I caress your body and kiss your skin
Our passion flows like summer rain
Our love's fulfilled as we kiss again.

In the afterglow
In fond embrace
We speak of love
And I kiss your face.

53. Keepsakes

I keep your beauty in my eyes
Your vision adorns my mind
I keep the taste of you on my lips
Your sweetness taints my palate.

I keep your fragrance in my nose
Where it pervades my senses
I keep your tender tones in my ears
Your laughter fills my heart.

I keep the touch of you on my skin
The warmth of you in my fingers
I keep the essence of you in my soul
I keep your love in the haven of my heart
Always.

54. Feelings

When I look into your beautiful blue eyes
I can see the stars twinkling in the skies
When I feel your hand touch mine
I feel a warmth so deep so fine.

You have stolen my heart
I begged my heart not to love from the start
I told my mind not to feel
So I wouldn't be blinded by something unreal.

Look at me now on a rollercoaster of love
Heaven sent you from above
You have set my world on fire
Throwing me into a whirlwind of desire.

How can I reason with my heart when it beats so?
How can I control my emotions' ebb and flow?
Tell me why I want you near
Tell me why I love you dear.

You were meant for me
You fill my every need
Are we only filling time
Or does destiny have us in mind?

You are always there when I need you
I hope you feel I'm there for you too
Two lonely hearts drinking the wine of woes
Holding each other tight while our love grows

You are my angel sent from above
To hold me and help me love
You make my heart soar like a dove
My beautiful angel my one true love.

55. Explain

I can't explain
The sort of pain
I feel inside
My heart and brain.

When you're not near
I tremble, I fear
My heart will break
Because you're not here.

Then I close my eyes
And I see
A picture of you
And it's plain to me.

How much we're in love
And how happy we'll be
When we are together
For all eternity.

56. Wishes and Dreams

I used to wish upon a star
I'd pray to heaven way up far
For an angel to descend
And want to be my friend.

I dare not think
I couldn't imagine
The love of an angel
So pure and lasting.

I saw you there
And my heart did soar
I've never felt before
A love so wonderful and so pure.

Now I stop and sometimes think
I'm so lucky I was on the brink
Of a life distraught with shattered dreams
Falling apart at the seams.

I thank the stars and heaven above
You filled my heart with pure true love
We'll be together forever you see
With a love in our hearts that is meant to be.

57. I Love

I love you when you're sleeping
I love you when you're awake
I get so excited when I see you
That I begin to shake.

I love to sit and snuggle
When listening to a CD
And love the fact that when I talk
You really listen to me.

I know that when I look at you
My eyes begin to shine
I love being part of your life
And you being part of mine.

I know that one day soon
We will be as one in life
Because that's the day I've waited for
Always all my life.

58. I'll Be There for You

Lately I've been trying to find the words
To prove my love is true
And no matter what happens in this world
I'll be there for you.

I'll be there for you when you need someone
To come and hold you tight
I'll be there for you even if you call
In the middle of the night.

I'll be there for you when the rain won't stop
Falling upon your life
I'll wipe your tears and chase your fears
I'll help you with your fight.

I'll do my best to protect you from harm
To keep you safe and well
And when you have a problem hidden
I'll be who you can tell.

I'll take your very darkest night
And I'll make it bright for you
And even if we are apart
My love will still be true.

And even if they send me away
To a hospital far away
I won't give up I'll fight for us
Every hour of every day.

When this world turns bitter and cold
And you don't know what to do
I'll be the one that's there to hold
Together we'll pull through.

When you're alone calling out for help
Struggling to even stand
I'll use my strength to keep you up
I'll hold out to you, my hand.

And I know these are but just words on a page
But they mean so very much more
They are everything that I promise to do
They are everything for you, I'd endure.

And I know I'm not as strong as before
And maybe now I'm a little weak
But my love for you stands as strong
Even when the world seems bleak.

You have given me a reason to live and fight
So I'll live and I'll fight for you
For I know together, even though we have suffered
In the end we will pull through.

All the pain you have been handed
You don't deserve a drop
You're not a bad person and you've done nothing
wrong
So I'll fight for your pain to stop

It makes me very angry that someone so pure
Should be made to feel this pain
I know that there's no miracle cure
But I'll try to stop this rain.

So when the world turns bitter and cold
And you don't know what to do
You'll never have to be afraid
Cos I'll be there for you.

59. Mother's Always Here

She'll always be with you
In your head and your heart
She'll always walk beside you
You will never part.

Look for her in your dreams
And I think you'll find
She'll always be there with you
Until the end of time.

Look into your memories
To a happier time
You'll find her face
Loving, caring and kind.

Remember a place at a joyful time
Memories of happiness are good for the mind
You'll see your mother with a beaming smile
Hugging and kissing you, as a child.

Your heart will soar with love and affection
When you remember Mother, always offered
protection
She'd be so proud of her little girl
As she was when she brought you into this world.

The strength of your character firm, kind and true
Are the things that she gave you, to see your life
through
As a strong loving mother with a strong will and
mind
Remember your mother loves you, for all time.

60. Vision

I can see a vision
A vision in my head
This vision is so beautiful
And laying on my bed.

I see your beauty in my mind
You're floating around my head
I love the way you look at me
I love the things you've said.

You're always in my heart
You're always in my head
And I know we'll never part
For each other we were bred.

To the future we both look
It's getting closer every day
Never a word mistook
I love you in every way.

When we are together
Forever, for all time
I know you know I love you
I'm glad you will be mine.

61. My Angel

Sleeping angel where are you now?
I want to see you but don't know how
I know you're with me in the day and night
I can see you in your dazzling light.

Sleeping angel you make my heart pound
I want to hear you but you don't make a sound
I know you're near me but I don't know how far
Your light is brighter than a shining star.

Sleeping angel come stay with me
I want you with me where ever I'll be
Gazing at me while I sleep
Nobody knows the secrets we keep.

62. Thank You

Thank you for giving a card to me
Filled with compassion and love I see
Thank you for loving, thank you for caring
Thank you for sharing your love with me.

The greatest gift I ever did see
Came from you specially for me
A wonderful vision I have to behold
Is all of your love mind, body and soul.

63. Near Tomorrow

When I'm without you
It doesn't seem quite right
I don't know just what to say
I'm awake most of the night

I awake in the morning
And begin to despair
When am I going to see you?
Life isn't really fair

Then I get to see you
Those amazing eyes and smile
It's enough to keep me going
For a short while

I have to live on daydreams
I have them every day
In them you are with me
And you're here to stay

I want them to be real
Wake up with you every day
Because the way I feel
There's not much more I can say

But in a near tomorrow
Next to me you'll lay
And I can say good morning
I love you in every way.

64. Courage

Courage is the strength to stand
When it's easier to fall
It's the conviction to explore
When it's easier to believe what we're told.

Courage is the desire to maintain our integrity
When it's easier to look the other way
It's the feeling to be happier and alive
When it's easier to feel sorry for ourselves.

Courage is the will to shape our own world
When it's easier to let someone else do it for us
It's the recognition that no one is perfect
When it's easier to criticise and abuse.

Courage is the power to step forward and lead
When it's easier to follow the crowd
It's the spirit that makes you climb as high as you
can
When it's easier to stay on the ground

The foundation of courage is solid
The rock that doesn't roll
Courage is the freedom of
Our mind, body and soul.

65. All the World to See

Only in your presence
It went from ear to ear
That beaming smile you're on about
Every time you are near.

I was very sad and lonely
I didn't really care
Then I saw an angel
Smiling with golden hair.

I looked into those amazing eyes
To see what I could see
Like a lightning bolt from the skies
I could see you were meant for me.

The looks and blinks and flickers and winks
Were difficult to disguise
Cos I could tell that you loved me
I could see it in those eyes.

Amazing beautiful angel
You saved my heart from hell
Can't you see it in my eyes?
I love you, can't you tell?

And now we are together
For all eternity
The love we share is in our eyes
For all the world to see.

66. No Promises

From this day forward
You shall never walk alone
My heart is my shelter
My arms will be your home.

I cannot promise you sunshine
I cannot promise riches, wealth or gold
I cannot promise an easy path
That leads from change of growing old.

But I can promise all my heart's devotion
A smile to chase away your tears
A love that's ever true and growing
And a hand to hold through all your fears.

67. You Are

You are my sun you are my moon
You are my words you are my tune
My earth my sky my sea
You are everything to me
You are the light in my darkness
You are my peace and my happiness
My hope and forever my love.

68. Over and Over

Only in my wildest dreams
Did I ever imagine a woman like you
One who'd meet my greatest expectations
And fulfil my most passionate desires.

Each tender moment we share draws me closer to
you
And I'm left with a feeling of complete satisfaction
Sometimes I tremble with anticipation
At the mere thought of you.

It's in that moment my desires overwhelm me
Only in my wildest fantasies did I ever imagine
It would be this way over and over and over again
You take my breath away.

69. With You

Make a wish and give it wings
Dream of bright and wonderful things
Dance through all our fun-filled hours
Make that Jovi song ours.

Share a love song for our sake
All life's joys are ours to take
And when the evening comes to view
I'll thank my lucky stars that I'm with you.

70. Loneliness

Surrounded by so many
But isolated and alone
I try to reach out to someone
But succeed in grasping none.

Struggling to keep my sanity
I plunge myself into darkness
It's the only place to hide
To cope with all inside.

It's draining wanting something you don't have
Each morning I wake with loneliness at my side
Each day I walk with its presence
Each night it lies with my insomnia.

Have I become invisible or a figment of
imagination?
They cried on my shoulders and I soaked up their
tears
But when I need someone
Where did they all go?

71. No Matter

No matter where you travel
No matter where you go
My love for you will follow
Just as the rivers flow.

No matter where life takes you
Be it near or far
Look up into the sky
And see the brightest star.

If that star is the first
We will see at night
Then make a wish and I will too
That soon we'll reunite.

No matter where you travel
We will never truly part
Because you see I carry you
Deep within my heart.

72. Miracle

Once in a lifetime
You find someone special
Your lives intermingle
And somehow you know.

This is the beginning
Of all you have longed for
A love you can build on
A love that will grow.

Once in a lifetime
To those who are lucky
A miracle happens
And dreams do come true

I know it can happen
It happened to me
For I've found my once in a lifetime
With you, you see.

73. Did I Mention?

Did I mention
That it's my intension
To give you a dose
Of sadness prevention?

Did I mention
Or did I say
My love for you
Will never fade away?

Did I mention
Maybe someday
I'll make you happy
Forever and a day?

Did I mention
I probably did
Forever with you
I intend to live?

Did I mention
I forgot to say
My love for you
Grows greater every day?

Did I mention
In a number of ways
I'll be with you
Forever, always?

74. I Could

I could watch the sun rise
I could watch the sun set
I could walk in the rain
Without getting wet.

I could witness their beauty
As the flowers bloom
I could feel the sunshine
Through the darkest clouds.

I could walk on water
Without soaking my feet
I could travel the world
In less than a week.

I could ponder the knowledge
Passed down from the wise
I could live in a castle
Built up in the skies.

I could paint a portrait
And bring it to life
I could sleep without pain
On the edge of a knife.

I could play a melody
To soften the mood
I could take all the bad
And turn it into good.

I could float on the breeze
I could fly on the wind
I could soar high in the sky
And leave the world behind.

I could travel the cosmos
And watch all life unfold
I could witness its power
So wonderful to behold.

But all of the wonderful
Things I could do
There's nothing in the universe
That compares to you.

I'll hold you in my heart
For all the rest of time
You're my living miracle
And baby you're all mine.

75. The One

You came into my life
Like the first rays of sun
I knew right away
That you were the one.

There was no need for words
Just a small simple smile
My heart fluttered
And was beating like a child.

But unlike the stars
I hoped you wouldn't be gone
I want you here at my side
Until the light burns from the sun.

I want you here as the love of my life
You're not going back, I won't let go
I love you too much
And want the whole world to know.

76. You Are

You are the sun in the sky
You are the light shining by
You are the breeze everywhere
You are the life I want to share.

You are what makes my day go by
You are the one I tell no lies
You are the one who makes me smile
I'll stand by you for all time.

Your smile lights up my day
You make my darkness go away
You're the reason I'm alive
And one day you'll be my wife.

77. Intention

As long as my words
Are refined and snappy
I know they will
Always make you happy.

It is not my intention
To make you sad
Cos if that happens
I'll feel so bad.

So my aim is not to make you blue
Cos it's not just your smile
That makes me head over heels
And totally in love with you.

78. My Search for You

Love is strong, love is true
I'm waiting for it, longing for you
The moon smiles, I see your name in the stars
But I couldn't read it, it was too far.

Destiny holds me in the palm of her hands
I need relief from this hot burning sand
I want to hold you and feel your touch
I've waited so long, this is all so much.

Sweetness abides in the clouds up above
Carry me there on your wings of love
The warmth that comes from the one you love so
In the dead of winter, Can make flowers grow.

I have a treacherous road to travel
Before the mysteries of life, I unravel
But you'll be with me forever, your love in my
heart
From the day we met and never to part.

79. Truly Feels

I love you more than all the planets
Revolving around the sun
I love you more than all the stars
From here to kingdom come.

I love you with every beat of my heart
That's pounding every time we part
I love you more than life itself
I'd die for you today.

And when I'm up there with the angels
You would hear me say
I'm glad I love you
With all my soul.

I'm watching you from above
Because now I know
How it truly feels
To be totally in love.

80. Picture in My Mind

Whenever I'm not with you
Whenever you're not near
I look inside my head and heart
And picture you so clear.

Whenever I'm upset or down
My smile turns to a frown
I picture you with that wonderful smile
And those eyes turn everything around.

You are a wonderful person
Kind and caring too
My heart just melts, everything it helps
Every time I look at you.

So I carry this picture
Of you, it's in my mind
And it will stay forever
With me, till the end of time.

81. Society

Society seems in a mess
Mothers cry, while fathers stress
To be polite it's a disgrace
As children mock you, to your face.

Every day the papers show
That crime and rape, did upward go
The things done in laboratories
Are stashed away in lavatories.

Drugs and sex aren't hard to find
It seems as if the world's gone blind
For what the people fail to see
It's messing up society.

As dads no longer head their home
And kids all sit and chat by phone
What once to all had been a home
Is looking like a war-torn zone.

No longer do you find that kids
Are playing in the park
For it's become a hideout place
For gangsters in the dark.

What once was right now seems so wrong
No more joy and no more song
As what this all was meant to be
Lies buried in a cemetery.

By telling you these things my aim
Is not to make you mad
It's just to tell another truth
Which soon, will make you glad.

Amidst the chaos of this world
To hurt despair and pain
And hate along with treachery
All done for selfish gain.

There's this one thing I know of
And believe with all my heart
That once we're both together
We'll never be apart.

82. Stay Calm

Stay calm when all around you
Seems to be unfair
Stay calm when you need to
Or it will drive you to despair.

Stay calm when things conspire
To keep you and I apart
Don't let it hurt you
Because it will break your heart.

Stay calm when you're crying
All alone in bed
It's then when you need to
Or it will wreck your head.

Stay calm when we meet
And you're stuck for words to say
If you could read my mind
You'll know I feel the same way.

83. I Love You

I love you, I love you
With all of my heart
I love you, I love you
Right from the start.

I love you, I love you
In every way
I love you, I love you
I'm here to stay.

I love you, I love you
I have to say
I love you, I love you
In the night and the day.

I love you, I love you
It's clear to see
I love you, I love you
For eternity.

84. Any Parent to Any Child

I would do just about
Anything you'd ask
For you there's nothing I won't do
There's no such task.

I would walk without my shoes
To the ends of the earth
I would give up anything I had
To teach you self-worth.

I would hold your hand
Every minute of every day
But I won't because I know
You need to find your own way.

I would surely bare the heartache
Of your first love that's real
Even though I can't
I would feel the way you feel.

I would sell my soul
If it would keep you happy forever
I would give my right arm
To keep us forever together.

I would run a hundred miles
Uphill in the rain
Just to guarantee
That you will never feel pain.

I would laugh with you
Even if I was sad
I would give you a smile
Even if I was mad.

I can only accept your mistakes
With a grin on my face
I will guide you with correcting them
But only at your own pace.

I will guide you through life
As this world can be quite wild
Just don't ever forget
That you will always be my child.

85. Exercise

If I was some weights
I wouldn't be too heavy
I wouldn't take my toll
You wouldn't pay a levy.

You'd move me up and down
In and out and round and round
Never putting me down
Until big muscles you have found.

I'd sculpt and mould your body's folds
Leaving no fat on it
Then I'd stand and look at you
My beautiful Adonis.

86. Pink Day

You wouldn't have to think
If every day was pink
Dull it's definitely not
And is cooler when it's hot.

Pink is your favourite colour
It's obviously no other
I like pink too
Never been keen on blue.

If I paint our room pink
It will be pretty, don't you think?
It will make you happy too
You'll be smiling the whole day through.

You'll be happy
Driving around
In a pink car
That I've found.

You'll be happier in future
When I become your tutor
Cos then you'll drive around
On a pink scooter we have found.

We'll be very happy together
We'll be in love forever
And always in every way
We'll have a wonderful pink day.

87. Shout and Sing

I'll make it very plain
I haven't gone insane
But I would shout and sing
From rooftops and such things.

Profess what I want you to know
Talk of how much our love will grow
Say lots of wonderful things
To see what joy that brings.

Because all throughout my life
Through all my trouble and strife
I've never felt the same
When I hear you calling my name.

It's wonderful and it's new
Sharing my heart with you
I never have before
Let anyone in to explore.

I'm happy and content
The time with you I've spent
You're wonderful, happy and kind
I want to be with you for all time.

88. Determination

My poems have helped me clear my mind
I'm in control now, well most of the time
They give me a good and clear view
All this has happened since I met you.

There are things for a long time I've wanted to do
Now I think I'm in a place where my mind is true
You've helped me to clear all the things in my head
They kept giving me nightmares and wishing I was
dead.

So I have to train now and plan it right
Cos I know I'll be in one hell of a fight
I'll need to train hard, you can help me too
Know when I do this it will be all for you.

I've wanted to do this for a very long time
I didn't have the confidence until you were mine
A battle it will be but I'm ready to fight
And I hope you will be there to watch me take
flight.

I'm going to tell you now if I can
But giving up smoking is part of the plan
So if I can do this I know it is on
I'm going to run in a full marathon.

89. *Keeping you Safe*

There's an angel watching over you
Keeping you safe from harm
He'll never ever leave your side
Until you're safe in my arms.

Angels watch special people
And I know you're one
You're kind, thoughtful and caring
You're charming, loving and fun.

And when I fight my demons
I know you'll be the one
That holds my hand and stands with me
Until all the darkness has gone.

So until we are together
And you're in these loving arms
The angel watching over you
Will keep you safe from harm.

90. Million

I love you from the inside
Of that there is no doubt
You've captured my heart
And you, I cannot live without.

You make me very happy
With you I want to be
We'll live a life of bliss
Together you and me.

We'll find a million reasons
For the stars to shine on us
We'll have a million answers
When people cause a fuss.

I'll tell them that I love you
And you'll say the same as me
Because we will be together
Forever you and me.

91. Magic Wand

If I had a magic wand
I'd wave it over our bond
So invisibly you would see
You and me are meant to be.

I'd cast a loving spell
So in your heart you could tell
Forever we will stay
In love in a wonderful way.

We'd speak from heart to heart
Knowing we will never part
When it happens and we're together
We'll know it's always and forever.

I love you, can't you see?
And I know you love me
Forever in my heart
Together, never to part.

92. It's You

When I'm in my darkest hours
Remembering all my evil deeds
There is no hearts and flowers
Only brambles and dried up weeds.

It's when the pictures
In my mind
Remind me of the blackness
Of all of human kind.

When all the deeds
I've done before
Are dark and wicked
With blood and gore.

I see a light, that shines so bright
It comes to me and joins my fight
It's hard to see that angel's face
It soothes and cools me and gives me grace.

It's when I don't know
What to do
The angel appears
Thank God it's you.

93. Very Sorry

I'm very, very sorry
For my vocabulary
Now you've really seen
What an idiot I can be.

I'm really, really sad
That my mouth can turn so bad
And come out with words
I didn't really mean.

I hope you will forgive me
For words I shouldn't say
Because I really do love you
Forever and a day.

94. Weather

Rain, hail, wind, snow
Will never stop me from wanting to go
To see the woman of my dreams
With shining eyes and a smile that beams.

Lightning, thunder and bitter cold
Will never prevent me from the love I hold
For you my love, with all my heart
The weather will never keep us apart.

And in the freezing cold of night
I'll comfort you, I'll hold you tight
And in the morning glow of sun
I'll keep you cool, we'll have some fun.

Be it hot or cool or cold
Whatever you need I'll behold
My love for you is icily clear
My heart grows warm, when you are near.

So whatever the future weather dictates
It's plain and clear I'll make no mistakes
Together with you in these arms you'll see
Truth, honour and love there'll always be.

95. Speaking

I speak to you
You speak to me
We always speak the same words
You and me.

We speak of love
Of hopes and dreams
Whatever we say
The same things we mean.

We speak to each other
Through our heads and hearts
We speak of a time
We will never part.

My heart to yours
And yours to mine
Saying that our love
Will last for all time.

We've no need to speak it
In our minds we know
That the love in our hearts
Will grow and grow.

There will come a time
I mean it, you'll see
When we'll be together
For all eternity.

96. I'll Love You

I love you more than life itself
I'll love you in sickness and in health
I'll love you forever I have to say
My love for you will never go away.

I'll love you in springtime
I'll love you in summer
I'll love you in autumn
I'll love you in winter.

I'll love you when I'm happy
I'll love you when I'm sad
I'll love you when I'm good
I'll love you when I'm bad.

I'll love you forever and ever you see
A love for all time, through eternity
A love that speaks from your heart to mine
A love that will last forever, for all time.

A love that I see in your eyes and mine
A love that we feel with bodies that entwine
A love that I feel is so wonderful and true
The love that I have is always for you.

97. Healing a Heart

All through my darkest hours
The hurt and pain came through
My deepest painful secrets
I told them all to you.

You listened without condemning
To the good and bad in me
I opened up my heart
To show the pain, you see.

You gave me love and friendship
The kindness in your eyes
Your shining gleaming smile
Made me think, life is worthwhile.

And now my heart is mending
It's happiness I see
A life with you in future
Is more than enough for me.

Your bright and shining eyes
The beauty of your stare
That wonderful dazzling smile
Tells me you'll always be there.

I love you now and forever
You healed my broken heart
I knew that when I saw you
Never ever, will we part.

98. Mention

Did I mention?
I forgot to say
I'll love you tomorrow
The same as today.

I love you awake
I love you asleep
I love you so much
At the knees I go weak.

I wish I was there
Right by your side
Always and forever
My love I can't hide.

Maybe one day
It will happen you see
Together forever
And all eternity.

99. Mothers

No wonder you are the A to Z of finesse
You're a wonderful mother and nothing less
Proud and happy you will be
When your son makes a full recovery.

I sit here and think selfishly
I miss you so much it hurts you see
But you have a job for a lifetime to come
That's how it is when you're a mum.

Caring for all your children is no mean task
"When ill who will help them?" I hear you ask
No need to worry about their care
A wonderful loving mum is always there.

Standing in the background watching from afar
A mum will always comfort them, cos they're her
little star
It doesn't matter how many, one or ten
A mother's heart is full of love for all of them.

All your love will comfort them when they are
down
And you're full of sadness, when you see their
frown
But you will pick them up again, you always do
Nothing but a mother's love, can be so true.

So as I said just earlier, it's no mean task
A mother's love is always there and will always last
No matter if you're sad or glad, I have to say
A mother's love is always there, every day.

100. Together We Can

In the fullness of time we will unite
And face the demons, that scare us at night
I will help you and you will help me
To defeat the demons we cannot see.

Whatever it is that scares us my dear
We'll face them together with a cold chill of fear
We'll stand and fight whatever it is
That holds us back, we'll face the abyss.

We may not win this long drawn-out fight
But together we'll try with all our might
The demons inside our head and our mind
Will never let go, I think you'll find.

So together we'll face each other's foe
We'll never give up, we'll never let go
We'll continue to struggle, as long as it takes
We'll stand back up, when we fall, through
mistakes.

But this I promise, I swear to you, my oath
We'll support each other, together, we both
What we cannot see, we'll fight in our mind
We'll be solid together, forever, all time.

The battle will continue until our dying day
But together we'll make it, I know it, some way
With the love in our hearts and the bond of our
souls
We'll help each other to attain all our goals.

16763771R00081

Printed in Great Britain
by Amazon